Fun for Kids & Parents

Playmore Inc., Publishers
and
Waldman Publishing Corporation
New York, NY

*All the recipes in this book must be done with parental
or other adult participation and supervision.
These recipes are not meant for children to do on their own.*

We would like to thank the following for their participation:

American Dairy Association
www.ilovecheese.com

BUSH's Baked Beans
www.bushbeans.com

Chicken of the Sea International
www.chickenofthesea.com

Dannon®
www.dannon.com or 1-877-DANNONUS

Dole® Food Company, Inc.
www.dole5aday.com or 1-800-232-8888

Gold Medal®
www.BettyCrocker.com or 1-800-328-1144

Idaho Potato Commission
www.idahopotato.com

National Pork Board
www.otherwhitemeat.com

Nestle USA, Inc.
www.VeryBestBaking.com

New York Apple Association, Inc.
www.nyapplecountry.com

Produce for Better Health Foundation®
www.5aday.com

Texas Beef Council
www.txbeef.org

Tyson® Foods, Inc.
www.tyson.com

USA Rice Federation
www.ricecafe.com

Crunchy Vegetable Burrito Banditos

Ingredients

1/2 cup shredded Dole® carrots

1/2 cup chopped Dole® broccoli

1/2 cup chopped Dole® cauliflower

2 Dole® green onions, thinly sliced

4 oz. shredded low-fat Cheddar cheese

1/4 cup nonfat ranch salad dressing

1/2 teaspoon chili powder

4 (7") flour tortillas

1 cup Dole® iceberg lettuce, torn into bite-size pieces

Steps

1. In a mixing bowl, combine carrots, broccoli, cauliflower and onions with cheese, dressing and chili powder.

2. Lay tortillas flat on the counter and spoon about 1/2 cup vegetable mixture and 1/4 cup of lettuce down the center of each tortilla.

3. Wrap the tortilla around the mix.

Bush's® Baked Bean Tacos Olé

Ingredients
1 (28 oz.) or 2 (16 oz.) cans of BUSH'S® Baked Beans
1 lb. lean ground beef
1 envelope taco seasoning mix
12 taco shells
Favorite taco toppings

Steps
1. In skillet, cook ground beef until browned; drain.
2. Bring to a boil and simmer for 8 to 10 minutes or until thoroughly heated.
3. Spoon bean mixture into taco shells.
4. Top with favorite toppings.

Trees in a Broccoli Forest

Ingredients

2 Dole® carrots, peeled

3 cups Dole® broccoli florets

4 cherry tomatoes

3 tablespoons parsley leaves

For Dipping Sauce

1/4 cup plain nonfat yogurt

1/4 cup light sour cream

2 teaspoons honey

2 teaspoons spicy brown mustard

Steps

1. To prepare dipping sauce, combine yogurt, sour cream, honey, and mustard in a small bowl.
2. Hold carrots against cutting board and trim off ends.
3. Cut each in half, crosswise, then lengthwise to make four pieces.
4. Arrange each plate by putting two carrot pieces side-by-side in the center.
5. Arrange broccoli around the carrots forming a cluster.
6. Arrange the tomatoes at the top of the plate.
7. Spoon dip around the base of carrots and sprinkle with parsley.

Tortilla Chicken Crunch

Ingredients

16-oz. container Dannon® Plain Yogurt
1-oz. package dry ranch seasoning mix
1-1/4 pounds chicken cut into fingers or chunks
7 cups tortilla chips crushed or processed to equal approx 2-1/2 cups of crumbs
1 cup prepared salsa

Steps

1. Preheat oven 400°.
2. Mix together the yogurt and the ranch seasoning mix.
   Reserve one cup of the yogurt mixture for serving.
3. Take remaining cup of yogurt mixture and toss with the chicken.
   Roll in tortilla crumbs and place on a lightly greased baking sheet.
4. Bake 15 to 20 minutes or until golden brown.
5. Serve chicken with the reserved yogurt mixture and salsa.

Tuna Twist Casserole

Ingredients

8 oz. uncooked corkscrew pasta
8 tablespoons margarine or butter
2 cups (8 oz.) frozen mixed vegetables, thawed
1 large clove garlic, minced
1 can (10-3/4 oz.) condensed cream of mushroom soup
1 cup milk
1-1/2 cups (6 oz.) shredded mozzarella cheese
1/8 teaspoon pepper
1 can (12 oz.) Chicken of the Sea® Chunk Light or
Solid White Tuna in water, drained

Steps

1. Cook pasta according to package directions; drain.
2. In a large saucepan or skillet, sauté vegetables and garlic in melted margarine or butter until vegetable are crisp and tender.
3. Stir in soup, milk, cheese and pepper and cook over medium heat, stirring frequently, until cheese is melted.
4. Stir in pasta and tuna. Cook until heated through.

Rotini And Cheese

Ingredients

4 cups (about 11 oz.) uncooked rotini or rotelle pasta
3 tablespoons butter, divided
3 tablespoons all-purpose flour
3 cups milk, heated
2 tablespoons Dijon mustard
1 teaspoon salt
3-1/2 cups (14 oz.) grated Cheddar cheese, divided
1/4 cup dry bread crumbs
Fresh parsley sprigs, optional

Steps

1. Preheat oven to 350°.
2. Grease 2-quart casserole or 13"x 9" baking dish with 1 tablespoon butter.
3. Cook rotini in salted boiling water until al dente (or firm); drain and set aside.
4. Meanwhile, heat 2 tablespoons butter in a medium saucepan over medium heat until melted. Slowly add flour; cook and stir 3 minutes. Gradually add milk and continue to stir; cook about 6 minutes until mixture boils and thickens. Stir in mustard and salt.
5. Remove from heat; stir in 3 cups cheese until smooth.
6. Pour over cooked rotini; mix well. Pour into prepared dish.
7. Combine remaining 1/2 cup cheese, bread crumbs and dash of salt. Sprinkle over top of casserole.
8. Bake about 30 minutes or until hot and bubbly.
9. Garnish with parsley, if desired.

SHAKE 'EM UP CHICK'N TATERS

Ingredients

4 Tyson® Fresh Boneless & Skinless
   Chicken Thigh Cutlets
2 medium potatoes, cut into 8 wedges each
1/4 cup margarine or butter
1/2 cup flour
1/4 teaspoon salt
Dash pepper

Steps

1. Preheat oven to 400°.
2. Place margarine in 15"x10" baking pan. Place in oven 1 to 3 minutes or just until margarine is melted. Set aside.
3. In large plastic food storage bag or shallow dish, combine flour, salt and pepper; mix well. Shake or coat potatoes and chicken in flour mixture.
4. Place in baking pan. Turn to coat with margarine.
5. Bake at 400° 30 to 40 minutes or until chicken is done and potatoes are tender, turning once. Insert an instant-read thermometer into the thickest part of the chicken. Internal temperature should read 180° when done.

GRAND SLAM FRIED RICE

Ingredients

3 slices bacon
2 eggs, beaten
1 teaspoon minced fresh gingerroot (optional)
1/2 cup sliced green onions
1 cup finely chopped fresh mushrooms
3 cups cooked rice, chilled
1 tablespoon soy sauce

Steps

1. Cook bacon in large skillet over medium–low heat until crisp.
2. Place bacon on paper towels to drain.
3. Remove 1 tablespoon bacon drippings from skillet, set aside.
4. Increase heat to medium. Add eggs to skillet. Cook, stirring until almost done.
5. Push eggs to side of skillet. Return 1 teaspoon bacon drippings to skillet.
6. Add gingerroot, onions and mushrooms.
Cook until mushrooms are lightly browned.
7. Add rice and soy sauce to skillet, stir all ingredients together
until thoroughly heated, about 5 minutes.
8. Crumble bacon and stir into rice.

MUNCHY-CRUNCHY CHICKEN

Ingredients

3-1/2 lbs Tyson® Fresh Skinless Chicken Drumsticks
  or 3-1/2 lbs Tyson® Fresh Chicken Thighs
  or 1 package Tyson® Fresh Pick of the Chix
1 envelope (1.2 oz.) roasted chicken gravy mix
1 egg
2 tablespoons water
1/2 cup herb-seasoned stuffing,
  finely crushed (about 1 cup)

Steps

1. Preheat oven to 375°.
2. Pour the gravy mix in a big plastic bag (the kind with the reclosable top). Put the chicken in the bag. Close it tightly, shaking well to coat the chicken with the gravy mix.
3. Crack the egg into a cereal bowl, then add water and stir well.
4. Put the stuffing crumbs in another bowl. Dip the chicken in the egg mixture, then roll it around in the stuffing crumb until totally coated.
5. Put the chicken on a baking sheet. Put into the oven and bake at 375° for 15 to 20 minutes.
6. Turn the pieces over and bake 15 to 20 minutes more until juices run clear when thickest part of chicken is pierced or temperature on instant-read thermometer reaches 180°.

Black Bean and Rice Medley

Ingredients

3 cups cooked rice, cooled to room temperature
16~oz. can of black beans, drained and rinsed
1 large tomato, seeded and chopped
1/2 cup shredded Cheddar cheese (optional)
4 green onions, chopped
1/3 cup prepared light Italian dressing
1 tablespoon lime juice (optional)

Steps

1. Combine rice, beans, tomato, cheese and onions in large bowl.
2. Pour dressing and lime juice over rice mixture and toss.
3. Serve at room temperature or chilled.

Tuna-chiladas

Ingredients

1 can (10-3/4 oz.) condensed cream of chicken soup
1/2 cup sour cream
1 can (4-1/2 oz.) chopped green chiles
2 tablespoons margarine or butter
1/2 cup chopped onion
1 teaspoon ground cumin or chili powder
2 cans (12 oz. each) Chicken of the Sea® Light or Solid White Tuna,
   well drained, flaked
10 (7") flour tortillas
1 cup (4 oz.) shredded Cheddar or Cheddar/Jack cheese
Chopped fresh parsley

Steps

1. Combine soup, sour cream and chiles; set aside.
2. In medium saucepan, sauté onion and cumin in melted margarine
   or butter until onion is tender.
3. Stir in 1/2 cup soup mixture and tuna.
4. Spread about 1/3 cup tuna mixture along center of each tortilla; roll up
   tortillas and place seam side down in greased 13"x9" baking pan.
5. Spread remaining soup mixture over tortillas.
6. Cover pan with foil and bake at 400° for 20 minutes;
   uncover and sprinkle with cheese.
7. Bake uncovered 5 to 10 additional minutes until cheese melts.
8. Garnish with parsley.

Smoky Chipotle Cheddar-Stuffed Pigskin Potatoes

Ingredients

8 baking potatoes (8 oz.), scrubbed
Butter
1 lb. lean ground beef, cooked and drained
1 cup hickory-flavored barbecue sauce
1 canned chipotle pepper (packed in adobo sauce),
   seeded and minced
1 teaspoon adobo sauce (from can)
8 oz. (2 cups) shredded Cheddar cheese
   (preferably smoked, sharp or combination of both)
1/2 cup green onions

Steps

1. Preheat oven to 425°.
2. Prick potatoes with a fork and lightly rub with butter.
3. Bake for 1 hour. Let cool slightly.
4. Cut potatoes in half length-wise; scoop out pulp (reserve for other desired use),
   leaving a 1/2" shell.
5. Combine ground beef, barbecue sauce, chipotle pepper, adobo sauce and half
   the Cheddar cheese (use disposable gloves when handling the peppers).
6. Fill potato shells with mixture. Sprinkle with remaining Cheddar cheese.
7. Place potatoes on baking sheet;
   bake 10 minutes or until heated through and cheese is melted.
8. Sprinkle with green onions.

CHICKEN OF THE CAESAR WRAPS

Ingredients

4 cups romaine lettuce, torn into bite-size pieces

1/3 cup creamy Caesar salad dressing

1 can (12 oz.) Premium Albacore Chicken of the Sea® Solid White Tuna in Spring Water, well drained

1/2 cup Caesar croutons

1/4 cup grated Parmesan cheese

4 (9 to 10") flour tortillas

Steps

1. Toss lettuce with Caesar salad dressing to coat. Add tuna, croutons and Parmesan cheese; toss to combine.

2. Spoon salad mixture onto each tortilla near one edge. Roll up tortillas beginning with edge nearest salad. Seal end with a small dollop of additional Caesar dressing.

3. Cut tortillas in half to serve.

Pork Tenderloin with Apples

Ingredients
2 lb. pork tenderloin
3 large garlic cloves, minced
1-1/2 tablespoons prepared mustard
1 teaspoon dried rosemary or 1 tablespoon fresh
1/2 teaspoon ground mace
1/4 teaspoon ground cloves
2 tablespoons apple juice
1 can (28 oz.) crushed tomatoes
3 large New York State Crispin apples

Steps
1. Preheat oven to 450°.
2. Place the tenderloin in a lightly oiled baking dish.
3. Mix the garlic with the mustard, rosemary, mace, and cloves. Spread over the pork.
4. Bake for 10 minutes, baste with the apple juice, and reduce the oven temperature to 400°.
5. Roast another 10 minutes uncovered.
6. Layer the tomatoes over the top.
7. Peel, core, and cut the apples into 1/2" slices.
8. Add to the tomatoes around the pork.
9. Bake for 20 minutes or until a meat thermometer registers 170°.

Tuna Pot Pie

Ingredients

1 can (12 oz.) Chicken of the Sea® Chunk Light or Solid White Tuna, drained and flaked
1 cup water
1 teaspoon (1 cube) chicken flavored bouillon
1 cup frozen vegetables
1 cup milk
2 tablespoons cornstarch
1/2 to 1 cup shredded Cheddar cheese
1 can (8 oz.) refrigerated crescent roll dough

Steps

1. In a medium saucepan, combine water, vegetables and bouillon. Bring to a boil; cook for two minutes over medium heat.
2. Dissolve cornstarch in milk; stir into vegetables and cook until thickened.
3. Stir in tuna and cheese.
4. Spoon mixture into four (1 to 1/2 cup) individual pie pans or casserole dishes.
5. Separate crescent dough into four rectangles; cut each rectangle into six strips. Attach topping by crisscrossing six dough strips over each pot pie and pressing down firmly; trim excess dough.
6. Bake pies at 375° for 15 to 20 minutes.

Jammin' Joe Bake

Ingredients

1 lb. lean ground beef
1 can (8 oz.) tomato sauce
1/4 cup ketchup
2 teaspoons mustard
1 cup Gold Medal® all-purpose flour
1-1/2 teaspoons baking powder
2/3 cup milk
3 tablespoons butter or margarine, melted
1 egg
More ketchup, if you like

Steps

1. Heat oven to 450°.
2. Cook beef in 10" skillet over medium heat, stirring a few times, until brown; drain.
3. Stir in tomato sauce, 1/4 cup ketchup and the mustard. Spoon into ungreased 8" square pan.
4. Stir flour, baking powder, milk, butter and egg, using fork, until mixed.
5. Pour over beef mixture, and spread evenly.
6. Squirt or spoon more ketchup in a zigzag design over the top.
7. Bake 18 to 22 minutes or until crust is light golden brown.

Shelly's Quiche

Ingredients

6 slices whole wheat bread, cut in half diagonally
1 cup (4 oz.) chopped turkey
1 cup (4 oz.) shredded American cheese
1/2 cup shredded carrots
6 eggs
1 cup low-fat milk
1/2 teaspoon dill weed

Steps

1. Set the oven to 375°.
2. Cut the bread crusts off and cut each slice in half diagonally to make 2 triangles.
3. Press each triangle all around the sides of a lightly greased 9" pie plate. Use the corners of the bread to make a jagged edge.
4. Press the rest of the bread over the bottom of the pie plate. Bake 5 minutes.
5. Sprinkle the turkey, cheese and carrots into the bread shell.
6. With a fork, beat the eggs, milk and dill weed in a medium bowl until well mixed.
7. Pour the egg mixture over the ingredients in the bread shell. Bake about 40 minutes.
8. Pull out the oven rack and insert a knife into the quiche halfway between the middle and the edge. If the knife comes out looking clean, the quiche is done. If it's not done, bake about 5 to 10 minutes longer.
9. Let stand 5 minutes out of the oven before serving.

Tuna Crunch Casserole

Ingredients

1 can (10.75 oz.) cream of mushroom soup
1/4 cup milk
1 tablespoon Worcestershire sauce
1/4 teaspoon pepper
2 cans (14.5 oz. each) cut green beans, drained
1 can (12 oz.) Chicken of the Sea® Solid White or
    Chunk Light Tuna, well drained and flaked
1 can (8 oz.) sliced water chestnuts, drained
1 can (2.8 oz.) French fried onions

Steps

1. In a two-quart casserole dish, blend soup, milk, Worcestershire sauce and pepper.
Stir in beans, tuna, water chestnuts and 1/2 cup onions.
2. Bake at 350° for 30 minutes or until hot.
3. Stir; top with remaining onions.
4. Bake five minutes.

Idaho Potato Turkey Burger Pie

Ingredients

1-1/2 pounds Idaho Potatoes, washed and thinly sliced
1/2 cup minced onion (optional)
12 oz. ground turkey (or ground beef)
Vegetable oil spray
1/2 cup barbecue sauce or ketchup (or a mixture of the two)
6 slices yellow, low-fat American cheese
Salt and pepper to taste (optional)

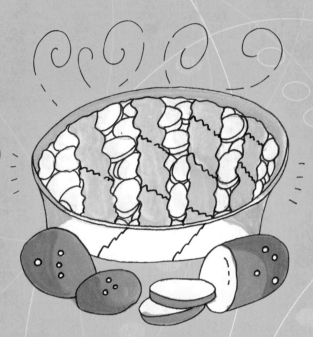

Steps

1. Preheat oven to 350°.
2. In a large, heavy stockpot, bring potato slices and 3 cups water to boiling. Boil, covered for 3 minutes or until potatoes are tender when pierced with a fork. Drain and set aside.
3. In a large frying pan with a lid, place onion (if using) and 1 tablespoon water. Cook onion and water over high heat with lid on for 2 minutes.
4. Add the ground meat and cook, stirring for 4 minutes, or until meat is browned and cooked through.
5. Spray a 9" deep pie pan with vegetable oil spray. Place 2/3 of the potato slices into the bottom of the pie pan; spoon the ground meat on top of the potatoes and drizzle the barbecue sauce on top.
6. Cover the meat with 4 cheese slices, cutting them to fit. If desired, season to taste with salt and pepper.
7. Cover the "pie" with the remaining potatoes, and top with the last 2 slices of cheese, cut into strips.
8. Cover pie loosely with foil, making sure that foil does not touch the top of the pie.
9. Bake for 20 minutes. Remove foil and bake another 10 minutes. Allow to cool 5 minutes before cutting and serving.

Chicken with Glazed Apples

Ingredients

4 skinless boneless chicken breast halves (about 1 lb.)
1/2 teaspoon ground nutmeg
1/4 teaspoon salt
1 tablespoon vegetable oil
2 cups sliced New York State Crispin apples
(about 2 medium-sized)
1/4 cup apple juice
1/2 cup apple jelly

Steps

1. Sprinkle chicken breast halves with nutmeg and salt.
2. Heat oil in 10" skillet over medium-high heat until hot.
3. Cook chicken in oil 15 to 20 minutes, turning once, until juice of chicken is no longer pink when centers of thickest pieces are cut. Stir in apples and apple juice.
4. Cook about 4 minutes, stirring occasionally, until apples are tender. Stir in jelly; cook and stir until jelly is melted.

Chili Potatoes

Ingredients

3 Idaho Potatoes (8 oz.), scrubbed
14~1/2 oz. can peeled whole tomatoes
19~oz. can dark red kidney beans, drained
7~oz. can whole kernel corn, drained
1 to 3 tablespoons chili powder

Steps

1. Cut potatoes in quarters lengthwise; then cut wedges into 1" pieces.
2. Over medium~high heat, bring a large pot of water to boil.
3. Add potatoes and return to boiling; cook for 7 to 8 minutes
or until tender. Drain well.
4. Return pot to the stove, reducing heat to medium.
5. Add tomatoes, breaking them up with a wooden spoon.
6. Add beans and corn.
7. Add 1 tablespoon of the chili powder; taste and add more if desired.
8. Cook until mixture is heated through.

APPLE MEATLOAF

Ingredients

2~1/2 lbs. ground beef
1~1/2 cups stuffing mix
2 cups finely chopped New York State apples
3 eggs
2 teaspoons salt
2 tablespoons prepared mustard
1 large onion, minced
3 tablespoons prepared horseradish
3/4 cup ketchup

Steps

1. Combine all ingredients, mixing thoroughly.
2. Pack into greased loaf pan 8"x5"x3" and bake at 350°
for 1 hour and 15 minutes.

Mild, Medium and Hot Idaho Potato Fries

Ingredients

6 large (8 to 9 oz. each) Idaho Potatoes, scrubbed
Cooking spray

Steps

1. Preheat oven to 500°.
2. Cut potatoes in half lengthwise.
3. Place each potato half, cut-side down, on cutting board and cut 1/4" lengthwise slices.
4. Place potato slices in a large mixing bowl and toss with desired seasoning mixture or salt and pepper to taste.
5. Line two baking sheets with foil and spray the foil lightly with cooking spray.
6. Divide potatoes between the two baking pans.
7. Bake potatoes about 10 minutes; remove from oven and turn over.
8. Return pans to the oven and bake another 10 to 15 minutes until potatoes are lightly browned and fork-tender.

Seasoning Mixtures for Mild, Medium and Hot Idaho Potato Fries

Onion Paprika Seasoning:

2 teaspoons paprika
1 teaspoon onion powder
1/2 teaspoon salt

Combine all ingredients in a small bowl. For a more spicy mixture, add 1/4 teaspoon cayenne pepper and/or 1/4 teaspoon ground white pepper.

Chili Seasoning:

1 teaspoon chili powder
1 teaspoon cumin powder
1/2 teaspoon salt

Combine all ingredients in small bowl. For a more spicy mixture, add another teaspoon of chili powder and/or 1 teaspoon crushed red pepper flakes.

Garlic Pepper Seasoning:

1/4 teaspoon garlic powder
1/2 teaspoon freshly ground
   black pepper
1/2 teaspoon salt

Combine all ingredients in small bowl. For a more spicy mixture, add another 1/2 teaspoon of black pepper and/or 1/4 teaspoon garlic powder.

Ham and Cheese Bakers

Ingredients

4 large Idaho Potatoes, scrubbed

2 tablespoons stick margarine, divided

2 tablespoons flour

1-1/2 cups evaporated skim milk

8 mushrooms, cleaned and chopped

1 small tomato, washed and chopped

1/2 cup diced smoked ham

1/2 teaspoon dried dill

6 oz. reduced-fat Cheddar cheese, shredded

Salt and pepper to taste

Steps

1. Preheat oven to 400°.
2. Prick each potato several times with a fork and place them on a baking sheet in the oven for 40 to 50 minutes.
3. While potatoes are cooking, melt half the margarine in a medium-sized saucepan over medium heat.
4. Whisk in the flour to make a thick paste.
5. Slowly add the milk and whisk until mixture is smooth.
6. Bring to a simmer and cook 2 minutes.
7. Add the mushrooms, tomato, ham and dill and cook another minute.
8. Turn off the heat and add the cheese, stirring until blended.
9. When potatoes are done, remove them from the oven.
10. Cut a lengthwise slit in each potato and open slightly.
11. Season potatoes with salt and pepper.
12. Serve each potato with one-fourth of the cheese mixture spooned on top.

VERY BERRY PORK CHOPS

Ingredients

4 pork chops, 3/4" thick
2 teaspoons vegetable oil
1/4 cup strawberry preserves
1 tablespoon mustard
1/4 cup cider vinegar

Steps

1. Heat oil in large skillet over medium-high heat.
2. Add pork chops, cook and turn until brown on both sides.
   Reduce heat to low.
3. In small bowl, stir together strawberry preserves, mustard and vinegar.
4. Pour sauce over pork chops. Cover pan. Cook pork chops
   for 10 minutes, or until the sauce has thickened.
5. To serve, spoon extra sauce over each chop.

Bush's® Barbecue Bean Cups

Ingredients

1 can (16 oz.) BUSH'S® Barbecue Baked Beans
1 can (12 oz.) refrigerated buttermilk biscuits
1/2 cup shredded cheese

Steps

1. Heat oven to 400°.
2. Place 1 biscuit into each cup of an ungreased standard-sized muffin pan.
3. Press dough firmly into bottoms and up sides of cups.
4. Spoon 1 generous tablespoon of beans into each biscuit cup.
5. Bake 11 to 13 minutes or until edges of biscuits are golden.
6. Sprinkle each bean cup with cheese.
7. Return to oven and heat 1 minute or until cheese has melted.
8. Let cool slightly.
9. Loosen edges of biscuits before removing from pan.

Easy Sausage Macaroni Supper

Ingredients

1 lb. mild Italian sausage or ground beef
1/4 cup chopped green or red bell pepper
1/4 cup chopped onion
2 cups (about 8 oz.) dry small elbow macaroni
2 cups water
1 cup Nestlé® Carnation® Evaporated Milk
1 cup chili sauce
1/2 cup (2 oz.) shredded mild Cheddar cheese

Steps

1. Cook sausage, bell pepper and onion in large skillet
until sausage is no longer pink; drain.
2. Stir in pasta and water. Cook, stirring occasionally,
until mixture comes to a boil. Cover; reduce heat to low.
3. Cook, stirring occasionally, for 14 to 16 minutes or until pasta is tender.
4. Stir in evaporated milk and chili sauce.
5. Remove from heat; sprinkle with cheese.
6. Cover; let stand for 5 minutes or until cheese is melted.

Just Peachy Peanutty Pork

Ingredients

6 boneless chops, trimmed, cut into 2"x1"x1" strips
1/4 cup peanut butter
1/4 cup peach jam
1-1/2 cups shredded coconut
3/4 cup graham cracker crumbs
2 teaspoons curry powder
1 teaspoon ground ginger
1/2 teaspoon ground black pepper

Steps

1. Heat oven to 400°.
2. Spray a 15"x10"x1" baking pan with non-stick cooking spray.
3. In small saucepan, cook peanut butter and jam over low heat until they melt together; remove from heat. Add pork and toss to coat.
4. In a large resealable bag, combine coconut, cracker crumbs, curry powder, ginger and pepper; shake well to blend.
5. Add pork to bag, a few pieces at a time; shake to coat.
6. Place pork in prepared pan and bake 8 minutes.
7. Turn and bake 8 minutes more, until coconut is nicely toasted.
8. Serve with hot rice or couscous and chutney, if desired.

Spaghetti Primavera

Ingredients
1 cup mushrooms, sliced
3 cups vegetables (see instructions below)
1 jar (28 oz.) low-sodium spaghetti sauce
4 cups spaghetti noodles, cooked

Steps
1. Vegetables can be any combination of broccoli, celery, onions, green or red bell peppers, carrots, pea pods, green beans, or others of your choice.
2. Mix all ingredients, except spaghetti, in a large pot, cover, and cook over medium heat for approximately 15 minutes or until desired tenderness, stirring occasionally.
3. Serve over cooked spaghetti.

Texas-Style Chili

Ingredients

2 lbs. sirloin steak, cut into 1/2" cubes
2 tablespoons vegetable oil
3 medium onions, chopped
2 cloves garlic, crushed
1 can (28 oz.) tomatoes, undrained
1 can (6 oz.) tomato paste
1 can (4 oz.) chopped green chiles
3 tablespoons chili powder
1 tablespoon ground cumin
2-1/2 teaspoons salt
6 whole cloves
1/4 teaspoon cayenne pepper, or to taste

Steps

1. In a Dutch oven, heat the vegetable oil over medium-high heat.
2. Add onions and garlic. Sauté until onions are tender, about 5 minutes, stirring occasionally.
3. Add cubed beef and cook until no longer pink.
4. Add the tomatoes, tomato paste, chiles, chili powder, ground cumin, salt, cloves and cayenne pepper.
5. Reduce heat to low.
6. Simmer, covered, for about 2 hours, stirring occasionally.

CINNAMON APPLE CHOPS

Ingredients

4 boneless pork chops (3/4")
Vegetable oil
1 teaspoon black pepper
1/2 cup chicken broth
1 tablespoon lemon juice
Chunky applesauce with cinnamon red hot candies *

Steps

1. Heat a non-stick skillet over medium-high heat.
2. Brush chops lightly with oil and brown chops on both sides, turning once, about 3 to 4 minutes.
3. Sprinkle chops with pepper, add broth and lemon juice.
4. Reduce heat to low, cover and simmer gently for 5 minutes.
   To serve, top with applesauce and cinnamon candies.

*In small saucepan, stir together 1-1/2 cups applesauce and 2 tablespoons candies.
Heat over medium heat, stirring often, until candies are melted; stir well to thoroughly combine.

Spinach Lasagna

Ingredients

2 cups low-fat ricotta cheese
1/4 cup fresh parsley, chopped
Non-stick cooking spray
2-1/2 cups low-sodium spaghetti sauce
1 lb. no-cook lasagna noodles
1 package (10 oz.) frozen spinach, thawed and chopped
1/2 lb. reduced-fat mozzarella cheese, grated
1/2 cup Parmesan cheese, grated

Steps

1. Mix ricotta cheese and parsley.
2. Coat a 13"x9"x2" baking pan with non-stick cooking spray; coat bottom of pan with a bit of the spaghetti sauce.
3. Place a layer of noodles over the bottom of the pan.
4. Cover noodles with about 1/3 of spaghetti sauce.
5. Spread half of the ricotta mixture over the sauce.
6. Spread half of the spinach over the ricotta, sprinkle with mozzarella. (If desired, you may add other vegetables to the spinach mixture.)
7. Repeat layers of noodles, 1/3 sauce, and remaining ricotta, spinach and mozzarella cheese, finishing with a layer of noodles, the remaining sauce, and a sprinkle of Parmesan.
8. Bake at 375° for 30 minutes or until hot and bubbling.

Terrific Turkey Tacos

Ingredients

1 teaspoon olive oil
1 cup onion, chopped
2 garlic cloves, crushed
10 oz. lean ground turkey
1/3 cup tomato juice
2 tablespoons chili powder
1/2 teaspoon cumin
Salt & pepper (optional)
6 (8") flour tortillas
3 cups lettuce, shredded
2 cups tomatoes, chopped

Steps

1. Heat oil in a skillet over medium heat.
2. Add onion, garlic, and ground turkey.
3. Cook until meat begins to brown. Drain any excess fat.
4. Stir in tomato juice, chili powder, cumin, and salt and pepper, if desired. Continue cooking, stirring occasionally, until the mixture is heated through.
5. Spoon onto warmed tortillas, top with lettuce, chopped tomatoes, and your favorite accompaniments: shredded low-fat cheese, avocado, or light sour cream.

Chicken-Asparagus Fajitas

Ingredients

1 lb. boneless, skinless chicken breast
1 tablespoon canola oil
1 lb. fresh asparagus, cut into bite-size pieces
1 cup green, red or yellow sweet pepper, sliced
1 cup onion, sliced
1/8 teaspoon cumin (optional)
1/8 teaspoon chili powder (optional)
1/2 cup salsa
6 flour tortillas
1/2 cup low-fat Cheddar cheese, shredded
   (optional)
1/2 cup fat-free sour cream (optional)

Steps

1. Wash chicken and cut into strips.
2. Heat oil in frying pan; add chicken and brown for about 10 minutes.
3. Add vegetables, spices, and salsa; continue to cook until vegetables are tender.
4. Place tortillas on microwave-safe plate and warm in microwave oven for 1 minute.
5. Place hot chicken and vegetable mixture in center of tortilla,
   top with cheese and sour cream, if desired, then roll tortilla.

All-Star Pork Meatballs

Ingredients

1 lb. ground pork
1 tablespoon onion flakes
3/4 cup crushed corn flakes
1/2 teaspoon salt
1/8 teaspoon ground black pepper
1 egg
1/4 cup ketchup
3 tablespoons brown sugar
1 teaspoon dry mustard

Steps

1. Heat oven to 375°.
2. In a large bowl, combine ground pork, onion flakes, corn flakes, salt, pepper and egg.
3. In a small bowl stir together ketchup, brown sugar and dry mustard.
4. Spoon 2 tablespoons of the ketchup mixture into the pork and mix well.
5. Spray muffin tin with vegetable cooking spray.
6. Form 6 meatballs and place in muffin tin.
7. Coat the top of each meatball with the remaining ketchup mixture.
8. Bake for 30 minutes at 375°, until nicely browned and glazed.

Alphabet Vegetable Soup

Ingredients

1 teaspoon vegetable oil
1/2 cup onion, chopped
1 clove garlic, crushed
2 cans (14-1/2 oz. each) reduced-salt chicken broth
1 can (28 oz.) crushed tomatoes
1/2 cup alphabet pasta
1 cup carrots, sliced
1 cup celery, sliced
1 cup corn kernels
1 cup green beans
2 tablespoons grated Parmesan cheese, optional

Steps

1. Heat oil in saucepan.
2. Add onion and garlic and cook until onion is tender.
3. Add chicken broth, tomatoes and pasta.
4. Bring to a boil, reduce heat, and simmer for 10 minutes.
5. Add carrots, celery, corn, and beans to soup and cook for 10 minutes.
6. Top with Parmesan cheese before serving, if desired.

Simple Spaghetti Squash

Ingredients

1 spaghetti squash (3 lbs.)
1/4 cup water
1 jar (32 oz.) low-fat, low-sodium
  spaghetti sauce

Steps

1. Cut squash in half lengthwise; discard seeds.
2. Place squash halves, cut side down, in baking dish; add 1/4 cup water.
3. Cover with plastic wrap and vent one corner.
4. Microwave on High power for 15 minutes, until squash is tender
   when pierced with a fork.
5. Scrape inside of squash with a fork to remove spaghetti-like strands. Set aside.
6. Heat spaghetti sauce in microwave until hot, 2 to 3 minutes.
   Pour sauce over cooked spaghetti squash.
7. To Bake: Place squash halves, cut side down, in a baking dish;
   add 1/2" water to dish. Bake at 350° for 45 minutes or until squash is tender.

Corn Chili

Ingredients

1-1/2 lbs. lean turkey, ground
1-1/2 cups onion, chopped
2 green bell peppers, chopped
2 tablespoons canola oil
1 can (28 oz.) crushed tomatoes
1 can (28 oz.) whole tomatoes
2 cans (15 oz. each) kidney beans
1 package (28 oz.) corn, canned or frozen
2 tablespoons chili powder
Rice (optional)

Steps

1. Brown the turkey in a non-stick fry pan over medium heat.
2. Sauté the onions and peppers in oil for 5 minutes until tender.
3. Drain the fat from meat and add to onion mixture.
4. Add the tomatoes, beans, corn and chili powder.
5. Cover and simmer for 1/2 hour.
6. If desired, serve over cooked rice.

CRISPY BAKED DRUMSTICKS

Ingredients

6 Tyson® Fresh Chicken Drumsticks
1/3 cup flour
1/4 cup fat-free egg product
   or 2 egg whites
1 tablespoon water
2 cups baked potato chips,
  coarsely crushed to equal 1 cup

Steps

1. Preheat oven to 350°.
2. Spray baking sheet with non-stick cooking spray.
3. Place flour in large plastic food storage bag.
4. In small dish, blend egg product and water.
5. Place crushed potato chips in separate shallow dish.
6. Add drumsticks to flour in bag; shake to coat evenly.
7. Dip a drumstick in egg mixture; coat evenly with potato chips and place on baking sheet.
8. Repeat with remaining drumsticks.
9. Bake at 375° for 30 to 35 minutes or until juices run clear when thickest part of chicken is pierced or temperature on instant-read thermometer reaches 180°.

Barbecue Pork Chops

Ingredients

4 boneless center cut pork chops, 3/8"
  thick
1/2 cup reduced-fat Italian salad dressing
1/2 cup barbecue sauce
1 teaspoon chili powder

Steps

1. In a small bowl, stir together Italian salad dressing,
   barbecue sauce and chili powder.
2. Place pork chops in plastic container.
3. Coat chops with 1/2 cup of sauce.
4. Cover container and marinate in refrigerator for 30 minutes or overnight.
5. Drain marinade from pork and throw away.
6. Heat non-stick skillet over medium-high heat.
7. Place pork chops in skillet and cook for a few minutes on both sides.
8. Pour the remaining sauce over the chops and cover the pan.
9. Turn heat to low and simmer for 5 minutes.
10. Serve immediately, topped with sauce.

Mexicali Beef Stew

Ingredients

2-1/2 lbs. beef for stew, cut into 1 to 1-1/2" pieces
2 tablespoons vegetable oil
2 large onions, chopped
4 cloves garlic, crushed
2 cans (14 oz. each) ready-to-serve beef broth
1 cup mild or medium prepared picante sauce
2 medium zucchini, thinly sliced
4 teaspoons cornstarch
1/4 cup cool water
2 small tomatoes, each cut into 8 wedges
1 can (2-1/2 oz.) sliced ripe olives, drained

Steps

1. In Dutch oven, heat oil over medium heat until hot.
2. Add beef, onions, and garlic, 1/2 at a time.
3. Brown beef evenly, stirring occasionally. Pour off drippings, if necessary.
4. Stir broth and picante sauce into beef mixture. Bring to a boil.
5. Reduce heat to low, cover tightly and simmer 1-1/2 hours.
6. Add zucchini to stew. Cover and continue cooking 10 minutes
   or until beef and zucchini are tender.
7. Stir cornstarch into the 1/4 cup water until smooth. Stir mixture into stew.
8. Bring to a boil over medium heat. Cook and stir 2 minutes or until thickened.
9. Stir in tomatoes and olives. Remove from heat. Cover and let stand 5 minutes.
10. Prepare a pumpkin shell by cutting top off of the pumpkin,
    scraping out and discarding fibers and seeds.
11. Boil water and pour to fill the pumpkin shell at least three-quarters full;
    cover and let stand for 10 minutes.
12. Pour water out of pumpkin.
13. To serve, ladle stew into pumpkin shell.

Spaghetti and Meatballs

Ingredients

1 package (16 oz.) heat-and-serve frozen beef meatballs
1 jar (30 oz.) prepared spaghetti sauce
Spaghetti or favorite pasta
Grated Parmesan cheese

Steps

1. Microwave frozen meatballs according to package directions.
2. Meanwhile, heat spaghetti sauce in large non-stick skillet over medium-low heat 10 minutes, or until heated through. Stir occasionally.
3. Add meatballs to sauce.
4. Serve over spaghetti or other pasta; sprinkle with Parmesan cheese if desired.

CHICKEN TACO TURNOVERS

Ingredients

4 Tyson® Fresh Boneless, Skinless Chicken Thigh Cutlets
2 tablespoons (half of a 1-1/4 oz. envelope) 40%-less-sodium taco seasoning mix
1/3 cup water
4 fat-free (8 to 10") flour tortillas
1/2 cup canned fat-free refried beans
4 oz. Mexican cheese spread, sliced or shredded

Steps

1. Preheat oven to 400°.
2. Spray baking sheet with non-stick cooking spray.
3. Cut chicken into 1/2" pieces.
4. Sprinkle 1 teaspoon taco seasoning on chicken.
5. Spray medium non-stick skillet with non-stick cooking spray.
6. Heat over medium-high heat until hot. Add seasoned chicken. Cook and stir 3 to 4 minutes or until juices run clear when thickest part of chicken is pierced or temperature on instant-read thermometer reaches 180°.
7. Stir in water and remaining (about 4 teaspoons) taco seasoning mix.
8. Bring to a boil. Reduce heat to medium and cook about 5 minutes or until very thick, stirring occasionally.
9. Meanwhile, spread each tortilla with 2 tablespoons refried beans.
10. Place 1/4 of the chicken mixture on half of each tortilla. Top with cheese.
11. Fold tortillas over to cover chicken and cheese, pressing down gently.
12. Place turnovers on baking sheet. Spray tops with non-stick cooking spray.
13. Bake at 400° for 5 minutes or until hot and cheese melts.

The BIG Burrito

Ingredients

1 lb. ground beef
1 package (1-1/4 to 1-1/2 oz.) dry taco seasoning mix
3/4 cup water
1 can (15 to 16 oz.) pinto beans, drained and rinsed
3 cups cooked rice
1/4 cup sour cream
2 tablespoons salsa
3/4 cup shredded Cheddar cheese
6 (10") flour tortillas

Steps

1. Put large skillet on burner over medium heat.
2. Cook beef until browned, about 5 minutes, stirring to break up beef into small pieces.
3. Remove skillet from heat; set aside.
4. Place strainer in sink; pour beef into strainer to drain fat.
5. Return beef to skillet and return to burner.
6. Add taco seasoning and water; mix well. Cook 2 minutes.
7. Turn burner off.
8. Add beans, rice, sour cream, salsa and cheese to beef; mix well.
9. Place tortilla on plate and spoon 1 cup beef mixture down center of tortilla.
10. Fold opposite sides of tortilla to center and roll tightly.
11. Place burrito on microwave-safe plate and cook on High power for 30 seconds.

Confetti Meatloaf

Ingredients

1-1/2 pounds lean ground beef
5 oz. fresh spinach, finely chopped
2 carrots, grated
1 tablespoon Worcestershire sauce
1 egg, beaten
3/4 cup vegetable or tomato juice (divided)
1/4 cup fresh Parmesan cheese, grated
1/4 cup fine dry bread crumbs
1/4 cup onion, finely chopped
1/4 teaspoon salt
1/4 teaspoon pepper
1/4 cup ketchup

Steps

1. Preheat oven to 350°.
2. In a small bowl, combine 1/4 cup of the vegetable or tomato juice and the ketchup. Set aside.
3. Combine all other ingredients and mix well.
4. Form into a loaf and place in a 1-quart loaf pan.
5. Bake in 350° oven for 50 to 55 minutes or until center of meat loaf reaches 160° on an instant-read thermometer.
6. Top with reserved juice and ketchup mixture during last 5 minutes of cooking.

Easy Cheesy Broccoli Rice Casserole

Ingredients
Vegetable cooking spray
3/4 cup chopped onion
3/4 cup chopped celery
3 cups cooked rice
1 package (10 oz.) frozen chopped broccoli, thawed
1 can (10-3/4 oz.) cream of mushroom soup
3/4 cup grated Cheddar cheese, divided
1/2 cup sour cream
1 teaspoon salt
1/2 teaspoon ground black pepper

Steps
1. Preheat oven to 400°.
2. Lightly coat large skillet with cooking spray.
3. Add onion and celery to skillet.
4. Over medium heat, cook vegetables until tender crisp, about 3 minutes.
5. Stir in rice, broccoli, soup, 1/2 cup cheese, sour cream, salt and pepper; mix well.
6. Remove skillet from heat and place on hot pad.
7. Lightly coat 1-1/2 to 2-quart baking dish with cooking spray.
8. Spoon rice mixture into baking dish.
9. Place rice mixture in oven; bake 35 minutes.
10. Remove rice mixture from oven and top with 1/4 cup cheese.
11. Return rice mixture to oven. Bake 3 minutes longer, or until cheese melts.
12. Remove from oven and serve.